Train Your Brain With Activities of Odds and Chance

THINK LIKE A
PROGRAMMER

by Emilee Hillman

illustrated by
Dana Regan

Published in 2020 by Cavendish Square Publishing, LLC
243 5th Avenue, Suite 136, New York, NY 10016

Website: cavendishsq.com

This publication represents the opinions and views of the author based on his or her personal
experience, knowledge, and research. The information in this book serves as a general
guide only. The author and publisher have used their best efforts in preparing this book and
disclaim liability rising directly or indirectly from the use and application of this book.

All websites were available and accurate when this book was sent to press.

Library of Congress Cataloging-in-Publication Data

Names: Hillman, Emilee, author. | Regan, Dana, illustrator.
Title: Train your brain with activities of odds and chance / Emilee Hillman ; illustrator, Dana Regan.
Description: First edition. | New York : Cavendish Square, 2020. | Series: Think like a programmer |
Audience: Grades 2 to 5. | Includes bibliographical references and index.
Identifiers: LCCN 2018058578 (print) | LCCN 2019000727 (ebook) | ISBN 9781502648099 (ebook) |
ISBN 9781502648082 (library bound) | ISBN 9781502648068 (pbk.) | ISBN 9781502648075 (6 pack)
Subjects: LCSH: Computer programming--Juvenile literature.
Classification: LCC QA76.6115 (ebook) | LCC QA76.6115 .H55 2020 (print) | DDC 005.1--dc23
LC record available at https://lccn.loc.gov/2018058578

Editorial Director: David McNamara
Editor: Kristen Susienka
Copy Editor: Nathan Heidelberger
Associate Art Director: Alan Sliwinski
Designer: Joe Parenteau
Illustrator: Dana Regan
Production Coordinator: Karol Szymczuk

Printed in the United States of America

Contents

Introduction

You want to be a computer programmer—great! The best programmers understand how to put ideas together and test results many times. They also know how to give and follow instructions. The activities in this book will help you understand key concepts of computer programming. Some examples are **simulations**, **conditionals**, and the odds or likelihood of events happening.

This is all part of **computational thinking**. Despite the name, this way of thinking doesn't need a computer! All you have to do is think about how to solve problems, one step at a time.

These fun activities will help you train your brain to organize information to solve a bigger problem. You'll also learn that some solutions work well while others don't. That is why it's important to understand and practice this thinking. This is how you learn to think like a programmer!

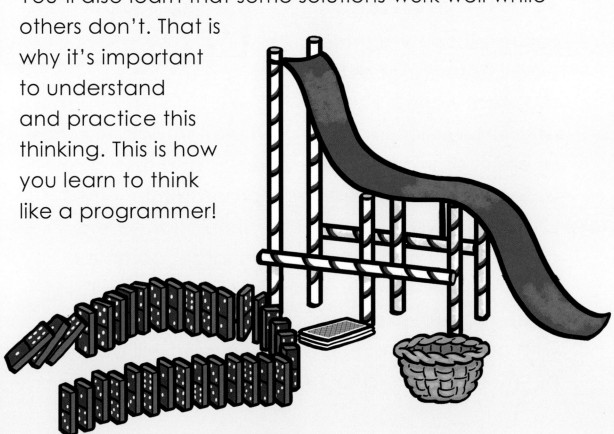

Simul-action!

NUMBER OF PLAYERS 2 OR MORE

TIME NEEDED

15–20 minutes

ACTIVITY OVERVIEW

You'll Need
- **Storybook**

To find out how a project works before it goes into the "real world," you can make a smaller version of it. This version is called a simulation. In computer science, simulations are designed and tested on a computer. They help tell a programmer if their program is working correctly. Simulations are a popular way of breaking down large, complex problems into smaller, more familiar **models**. Using these models, expert programmers can come up with new solutions! In this activity, you will act out, or simulate, your favorite book or story.

INSTRUCTIONS

You and your friends will choose a book with a story that you know well. Look over the book and plan how to act out each part of the story. Each of you can play a different character. Then act out the story. That way, you'll have a physical representation of the words on the page!

Simulation Charades

NUMBER OF PLAYERS **3 OR MORE**

TIME NEEDED

20–30 minutes

ACTIVITY OVERVIEW

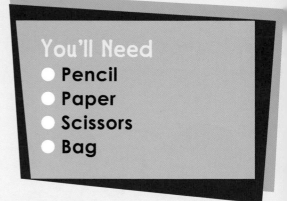

You'll Need
- Pencil
- Paper
- Scissors
- Bag

Simulations are helpful for **coders**, but they aren't always easy to understand. A good computational thinker is able to tie a simulation back to the larger issue. They will be able to solve the problem more easily because of the model. In this activity, you and some partners will try to figure out how to understand simulations.

INSTRUCTIONS

Have everyone work together to come up with a list. The list should have about ten activities on it.

Some examples are baseball or reading. Cut out slips of paper and write one activity on each piece. Fold the slips and put them into a bag. One player will draw an activity from the bag and act it out for the others. The person can't use words, though! The first person to guess the action correctly will score a point. Then the next person will pick from the bag and act out the word they get. Do this for all players until all the activities have been used. The person with the most points wins.

Conditional Seed

NUMBER OF PLAYERS

TIME NEEDED

15–20 minutes

You'll Need
- **Drawing supplies**
- **Paper**
- **Sunflower seed** (optional)

ACTIVITY OVERVIEW

Computer programs have a lot of instructions. Some of the simplest are if/then statements. These statements say IF something is done to a computer program, THEN the program will respond in a certain way. The if/then statements are also called conditionals. Conditionals are very powerful tools in computer programming. Conditionals are used in many different **computer languages**. In this activity, you will try to imagine what happens to a seed in the ground.

INSTRUCTIONS

Ask your parent or teacher for a sunflower seed. (If you can't get a sunflower seed, imagine you have one.) Then, draw pictures that show what you think will happen to that seed if it is planted in the ground. What will it look like as a **sprout**? What will the flower look like when it is fully grown? Will it grow tall? Imagine every stage of the growth process for the seed!

THINK ABOUT IT!

In computational thinking, it is good to test your ideas. You can test if your drawings were right by planting the seed. Take care of it. Watch it grow. What happens when you water it? What happens when it is in the sunlight? Were your drawings right? What do you think would happen if you forgot to water it?

Astronomical If/Then

NUMBER OF PLAYERS ①

TIME NEEDED

15–20 minutes

ACTIVITY OVERVIEW

Many rules computers use are based on ideas in nature or science. Computer programs use a lot of if/then statements. If/then statements can be used not just in programming but also in the real world. For example: IF it gets cold, THEN some birds will fly south. In this activity, you will try to come up with if/then statements that define the moon and the sun in the sky.

INSTRUCTIONS

First, check the exact time of day or night. Write that time on your sheet of paper. Then, see if you can find the sun or the moon in the sky. Draw what the sky and area (trees, grass, buildings) around

you look like right now. After you're done, think of some if/then rules that go with the time of day and the location of the sun or the moon. For example, "IF it's noon, THEN the sun is probably as high up in the sky as it will go."

THINK ABOUT IT!

Computer programs have lots of instructions. The instructions are called code. Many lines of code make up a program. There are lots of rules in a computer program, just like there are lots of rules in nature. One way you can build on this activity is to start writing down information on the location of the sun or the moon over a long period of time. Examples can be a week, a month, or a few months. This might help you come up with longer, more difficult if/then statements, such as "IF it's July, THEN the sun is out for a long time." What do you notice about your records?

Star Projection

NUMBER OF PLAYERS ● 1

TIME NEEDED

20–30 minutes

ACTIVITY OVERVIEW

Computational thinkers like to use simulations a lot. That's because simulations help them think through a difficult problem. They often make things easier to understand. They can also highlight unique parts of a problem. In this activity, you will simulate the stars.

INSTRUCTIONS

The best time to begin this activity is at night. First, draw your own **constellation** on a black piece of paper. A constellation is a special map of stars that looks like an object or an animal. Next, carefully poke a hole in your paper at the point of each star in your constellation.

Once you have finished making your constellation paper, pick a room in your house that can get very dark when the lights are off. Turn off the lights. Then shine a flashlight behind your paper. This simulates the way your constellation would look in the night sky.

THINK ABOUT IT!

There are many constellations in the night sky. Try looking up a map of them online. Then go outside on a clear night and try to find one. What is your favorite constellation? You can repeat this activity using your favorite constellation.

Constellation Interpretation

NUMBER OF PLAYERS **1**

TIME NEEDED

15–20 minutes

ACTIVITY OVERVIEW

Creating code is tricky, even for expert coders. If a coder forgets to leave a note while they're coding, someone else reading the code later might have a tough time trying to interpret their work! A good computational thinker breaks down a program and tries to figure it out. In this activity, you will connect the dots of a constellation.

INSTRUCTIONS

Before you begin, copy the constellation drawing in this activity onto a separate sheet of paper. Then, connect the dots of the constellation. What

shape appears?
Does this shape
match the name
of a constellation
in the sky? What
would you name the
constellation if you
saw it in the night sky?

THINK ABOUT IT!

Though code is tough, constellations are sometimes even more difficult to interpret. Trying to identify them, however, is a great way to learn about computational thinking. This type of thinking always tries to go beyond what is immediately obvious. To extend this activity, think of your favorite sport, book, or video game. What would your favorite athlete or character look like if they were a constellation? Draw an outline of the constellation first, then fill in the stars that would help someone identify it.

Egg in a Basket

NUMBER OF PLAYERS

TIME NEEDED

30–45 minutes

ACTIVITY OVERVIEW

A first attempt at solving a problem isn't always the best one. Computational thinkers and coders understand this. They make their first effort and observe what happens. Based on their observations, they make changes before trying again. Thinking like this will help you improve your solution and make it better. In this activity, you will try to protect an egg.

INSTRUCTIONS

Design a container to protect an egg that you will drop. Ask an adult for some different materials

You'll Need
- Pencil
- Drawing supplies
- Paper
- Building materials (such as Styrofoam, cardboard, construction paper, etc.)
- Plastic egg
- Egg
- Plastic bag

to build with. Explain to them it is to protect an egg. When you have your materials, think about what you will build. You should sketch out your ideas. Think about how your container will work.

Test your first drop with a plastic egg. Place it in your container and drop it with your arms out. Did it fall the way you expected? Do you see something you did wrong? Anything you could improve? Go back to your sketch and try again! Keep doing this until you think your container can protect a real egg. Then ask an adult for an egg. Put it in a plastic bag to avoid a mess! Drop it the same way. Did the egg break or not? Think about how the practice drops helped you improve your container. Improve it some more if you can!

Slide Design

NUMBER OF PLAYERS

TIME NEEDED

20–30 minutes

ACTIVITY OVERVIEW

In all projects they work on, computer programmers have to test their ideas. They do this by simulation as well as by building models. Models are different versions of the program. Sometimes they test the model in different situations. Many times, tests help programmers improve their programs. In this activity, you will build a model of a playground slide and test its structure with toys.

You'll Need
- Drawing supplies
- Paper
- Small toys
- Building materials (such as Styrofoam, cardboard, construction paper, etc.)

INSTRUCTIONS

To begin, think of a design for a new slide at your school's playground. Then, draw the slide. What makes your new slide design more fun than the one on the playground now? Using building materials like Styrofoam, cardboard, or construction paper, build a model of your design. Once your model is built, test it out using small toys. Can it stand under the test weight? Where can you make changes so the slide is safer?

Favorite Numbers

NUMBER OF PLAYERS

TIME NEEDED

5–10 minutes

ACTIVITY OVERVIEW

When programmers are first beginning to build a model, they have to try it out many times before they can find the code that does what they want it to do. It might take three tries, or thirty, or one hundred! In this activity, you'll test out how long it takes you to get the right outcome using dice.

INSTRUCTIONS

Pick your favorite number from 1 through 6. Throw one of the dice and mark on your paper if you got your number. Keep trying until you get your number five times, marking each throw on your paper. How many times did you have to throw the die in total?

Would it be easier to land on your favorite number if you threw both dice? Or would it be harder? Why?

THINK ABOUT IT!

"Odds" refer to how likely it is that something will happen. When you roll a die, you are just as likely to get a 2 as you are to get one of the other numbers. Because a die has six sides, we say that the odds of rolling a 2 are "one in six." That means that if you roll a die six times, you will probably only get a 2 once. However, odds are only a guess. They tell you what will *probably* happen, not what will *definitely* happen. You might get a 2 all six times! But it isn't very likely.

Fun with Playing Cards

NUMBER OF PLAYERS 2–3

TIME NEEDED

10–20 minutes

ACTIVITY OVERVIEW

When programmers are testing things out, some outcomes are more likely than others. In this activity, you'll try to get different outcomes using a deck of cards.

INSTRUCTIONS

One of you will be the dealer. The other players will each pick one of the four **suits** (diamonds, hearts, clubs, or spades). The dealer will give six cards to each person. Whoever gets the most cards of their suit wins that round.

Try it again with a different person playing the dealer. This time, the other players should each pick a different number from 2 to 10. The dealer hands everyone six cards. Whoever gets the most cards of their number wins. Did you get more cards of your suit in round one or of your number in round two? Why do you think that is? Count how many cards in the whole deck are of your suit and how many are of your number.

A Maze in Dominoes

NUMBER OF PLAYERS **1**

TIME NEEDED

5–10 minutes

You'll Need
- **Dominoes**

ACTIVITY OVERVIEW

When computer programmers create if/then statements, they need to be very clear so that the computer knows exactly what to do. For example, IF you flip a light switch up, THEN the lightbulb turns on. But if the wires between the light switch and the lightbulb aren't connected correctly, the bulb won't be able to go on. In this activity, you'll think about if/then statements while playing with dominoes.

INSTRUCTIONS

Set up a maze of several dominoes standing up in a row. Then try pushing the first one over. Did the others fall over? If not, why not? Try again. You're

trying to make it so that IF you hit one domino, THEN the others fall down. Maybe in one test, IF you hit one domino, THEN only one more follows. How can you adjust your domino pattern so that more of them will fall? Experiment with the distance between each domino.

Hopscotch

NUMBER OF PLAYERS 2 OR MORE

TIME NEEDED

10–15 minutes

ACTIVITY OVERVIEW

Coders can use different programs or commands to get the same results. Maybe one program is best for building a video game. However, it doesn't work very well for illustration. Coders test them out to use the best tools to make the final product. In this activity, you and your friends will try different versions of hopscotch.

You'll Need
- Chalk
- Stone
- Safe area like a sidewalk, driveway, or walkway

INSTRUCTIONS

One of you will be the first to draw a hopscotch court. Each of you will take a turn throwing the stone and hopping through the squares to get to it. Then the next person gets to design the court. Try to come up with a different design than the first one. After playing each version, think about the differences between them. Which one was the hardest to play? Why? Think about the number of squares created in each hopscotch court. Which one would you choose if you wanted to finish really quickly? Which one would you choose if you had a sore foot?

Glossary

CODERS Another word for computer programmers.

COMPUTATIONAL THINKING A way of thinking where you break a big task into smaller tasks.

COMPUTER LANGUAGES Different ways of writing code that computer programs follow.

CONDITIONALS Rules that state what will happen if certain steps are taken. They are also called if/then statements. For example, IF I flip a light switch, THEN a light will turn on.

CONSTELLATION A group of stars in the night sky. They make a picture.

MODELS Versions of a program or design.

SIMULATIONS Set-ups that test different computer programs before they are final.

SPROUT A flower that is just starting to grow.

SUITS The symbols on playing cards—diamonds, clubs, hearts, spades.

Find Out More

BOOKS

Karanja, Caroline. *Gabi's If/Then Garden*. Code
    Play. North Mankato, MN: Picture Window
    Books, 2019.

Prottsman, Kiki. *My First Coding Book*. New York:
    DK Publishing, 2017.

WEBSITE

Kano

https://kano.me/articles/coding-for-kids

Coding company Kano's official website explores
coding for kids.

VIDEO

What Are Conditional Statements?

https://www.youtube.com/watch?v=h2qpa0d6ktU

This video explains conditions, or if/then statements,
and how they work on a computer and in real life.

Index

Entries in **boldface** are glossary terms.